Twenty-One Steps Further Away

Jennifer Pagni

BookLeaf Publishing

India | USA | UK

Presentation by *BookLeaf Publishing*

Web: www.bookleafpub.com

E-mail: info@bookleafpub.com

ISBN: 9789358317961

First edition 2023

DEDICATION

For my lil big miss and lil lil miss, you are my world, moon, and stars. You both push me to be the best me I can possibly be daily. You remind me to stay curious and to always explore this life worth living. I am so blessed you picked me. I hope you always know it's you who has the power and control to be anything you want to be. Stand tall, grow, and evolve always. I love you 🩶

ACKNOWLEDGEMENT

I couldn't have done this without Sarah, Zoey, Mimi, Miss Stacey, and my numerous family and friends. The incredible amount of support that came when I posted on social media blew me away. Complete strangers who understood exactly what I was going through, motivated me to keep writing. Showing my vulnerability helped me realize how I was never alone on this journey. Ryan, you are my biggest cheerleader…I would have never started this project without your motivation and push, just to be me. I can't thank you enough for your ears, eyes, intelligence, and humor during my most trying times…forever my rock. And thank you, beautiful reader…for reading along on this journey. I hope you know how strong and glorious you are.

PREFACE

"I will cut adrift—I will sit on pavements and drink coffee—I will dream; I will take my mind out of its iron cage and let it swim—this fine October."
Virginia Woolf

Bringing Awareness to Your Breath

I yearned for unrealistic illusions of a fulling life
Brimming with your praises and forsaken
embrace
Companionship and unity I have ached for
Hot cocoa with tiny marshmallows, love, and
desire
Warmth of family on a frosty Christmas morning
False hopes and bread crumbs of validation
Clashed forcefully into illusions of grander
Versions of you unseen, the flags posted
divergent from before
Victim or Hero, each chronicle you effortlessly
orchestrated
Piece by piece I relinquished my love, light, and
magic
Disenchantment has always been your specialty
Lagunitas leaves you boisterous and unsatisfied
A wicked Diabolist, full of delusions of
grandeur

Siphoned my soul and self worth to the dregs
Engulfed in darkness, my own cold abyss of
sorrow

Despair and anguish. Briny tears ruptured all
boundaries
Sweeping my limits into the corners of my
fragile recesses
Uprooting me off the illogical pedestal you so
fondly placed me upon
Consuming all purity, confidence, and
tenderness
A windbag of false aspirations, nothing tangible
ever achieved
Lost the most important core beliefs, misplaced
in the mist of gloom

It took awareness to my breath, to smell the
cauterization
The emanation of smoke within my fog of
despair
Your destruction of my essence laid the
foundation of clout
Determination and comprehension for rebirth
was mandatory
Hate and loathing emerged with each nip of the
sauce
Manure born from the rhetorical pompous
manhandling
Nurtured my magnifying growth of off path
mutation
Fruition of my need for self love full of grace

I am worthy of the love, light, and magic within
my soul and body
I am done being dilapidated by your conceited
heart.

Self Worth and People Pleasing

Subdued my twinkle to allow others radiance to illuminate
Their brilliance scorching my cheeks, as they jostled past my soul
So, I began to shrink, constrict, and deflate myself
Allowing them the capacity and my space...I thought vital to them
To be who they needed to be, at expense of my own worth
Look how glorious they can be at the price of my self respect

Sacrificing, it became so easy to put everyone first
My mold determined by others wants and needs
People pleasing morphed into my super power
Saving the day, fawning at my own detriment
Each unfurling of the cape received a smile
False sense of security created, losing myself in the process

Lost and Found

Finally awoke, utterly oblivious of who I was
Glimpses sprinkled here, dusted there...
But this morning it became blaringly apparent
Brain aggressively taps the backs of both
eyeballs
uh hello…tap…tap tap…Who the fuck are
you?!?
Rather alarming when you have no sense of self
Oh…but there is plenty of soul and grace
I am a mother, daughter, sister, friend, survivor,
save-the-day-er
But who am I? What is my purpose?
What do I stand for? What no longer fulfills me?
Brain is unhappy with more questions then
answers
And I am thinking too fast to even comprehend
My feeble attempt at a previous answer
But I do know and this is for certain
This time around, I will be found
And it starts small, a visceral reaction here
Knowing my weather pattern there…
Sometimes, even meeting myself for the very
first time
Creating an uniquely, magnificent, one of a kind
me
At least I know how I like my fucking eggs.

Momma Backpack

Carry me...Mom...up please?!
Momma Backpack...I need a squeeze!!
Pure sigh of content, her pint-sized body
unwinds
Mom, your cozy...fills my heart, as it reminds
Me...in my flawed beauty, mismatched pieces,
patched with grace
That I am, in fact her sanctuary, a safe space
Hey can I call you back, not tonight, tomorrow
afternoon?
Mac & cheese to make, then bubble bath, and at
least one tune
While I rub her back and once again try to make
her aware
Just how spectacular, one-of-a-kind she is, no
one to compare!

2 am Texts, a Duet

Filled with liquid courage
Convenient for you at 2 am
Venom burns with the nostalgia
As you...taught me hate
When love was all I wanted
Strived to always please
To be the best for you
As you floated to the top
At everyone's expense
Furnishing anything I could
Not ever enough for you!
Your projections of hate & shame
Drenching me savagely
When I think about it now
I wonder how you can even begin
To heal, grow, perhaps evolve
When you mock my growth
2 am texts remind me of
Laps of misery
Digs of short comings, depressed personality
When I only asked for communication
About our under the weather child
2 am text is how I reply, next night
Just thought you should know
Our little lady is up sick, not feeling well

It's Okay To Not Be Okay

Moments of despair, misery
Feel agonizing, literal pain
Playing games with our heads
Fog rolling in with such steam
Forest shrinking into single trees
Depression's rapid growth leaves us
Believing we are alone with no hope
Deceiving thoughts hold us prisoner
Leaving us feeling this will last forever
Chaos filled with lies and untruths
Sadness can last 240 times longer
Then any other emotions we feel
Rumination leaving us looping
Coils of thought intruding
Shoulda, coulda, just...
All self judgments, misconstrued
I just wanted to let you know
You are not alone, not this time
And this will not last forever
I will sit here beside you
Until the fog dissipates
And your brain clears...enough
To know it's okay to not be okay
Waves of emotions receding
This is a life worth living

Ups and downs, or downs with ups
This world is yours to discover, be apart
You growing, being the best you can be
Becoming your true unique, glorious self
This is what this life is about

Tomorrow is a New Day

Today I didn't finish what I started
My to-do list seemed so daunting
Sometimes I don't meet my expectations
Most times I fall a little short
When did I become so hard on myself?
Today I felt like I wasn't enough
Enough of what? That I'm unsure of...
But I know I didn't check that box
I am positive one thing is certain
Tomorrow is a brand new day
A fresh start, clean slate
Where I can try and try again
Perhaps a bit of rest and with grace
I can hush the harsh self judgment
Learning to be free of that part of me
I am enough. I am loved. I am glorious!

Uncomfortable Emotion Wheel

That overwhelming anger extruding
All those sentiments brewing
Might they be…perhaps
A number of diverse emotions
Scrambled into quite a mess
Bitter, harassed, frustrated
A dash of pressured and violated
Touch of infuriated with betrayal
A generous squeeze of let down
Season to taste with outrage
Your masking the anger again
Shallowing it down, that's in the past
Now you have created your own safe place
Fight, flight, freeze or fawn
While I can't say they are all gone
The time has come to repair and rest
Growing and even exploring those suppressed
Uncomfortable emotions that are valid
It's time to surrender, time to feel
With kindness and understanding
We start to heal

Same Soup, Different Bowl

Same old me comes and goes
Glimpses in the mirror, window reflections
Only out of the corner of my eye, am I familiar
My voice sounding identical, every now and
then
Surprises me with clarity, strength, and hilarity
My words have changed, new vocabulary
Different boundaries established in 2023
Some permeable, others impassable
Each one created with careful consideration
The versions of me, created to deal with the
trauma
Cheer and wave on the sidelines, some cry
Knowing I cannot bring them along for the ride
Each day growing, changing, evolving to be
The best possible version of me

It's Spooky Season A to Z

Autumn ushers in a brisk crispness to the air
Bewitching the senses with its sweet putrid
decay
Cackling fires, smoke lingers from the chimneys
Dusk abruptly creeping up, rushing our days
Enchanting pumpkin spice seemingly
everywhere
Frankenstein and 6-foot Skeletons preparing for
display
Grim Reaper on the move, a berobed personified
force
Horror Movie marathons, or perhaps some
Hocus Pocus
Invisible influences should be approached with
morbid curiosity
Jack-o-lanterns slowly creeping in with their
toothy grins
Knocking on the neighborhood doors seeking
trick or treats
Lurking in the night, little monsters & witches
deliver shrieks of delight
Mazes of corn to explore, apple and pumpkin
picking galore
Nocturnal spirits awaken with great zest and
animation

Orange, yellow, and red leaves dip and dive off
the glorious trees
Potions and elixirs bubbling in the caldron with
mysterious delight
Quest for the ultimate Halloween scare, no need
to beware
Resurrecting ghouls and ghosts with each ritual
Spine-chilling apparitions perched beyond the
veil
Tombstones seemingly springing up here and
there
Undead awaiting for reanimation with jubilation
Voodoo magic with guiding spirits fills the
atmosphere
Wizards and warlocks clamor for power
Xenagogue guiding us through the house of
horrors
Yells and yelps of terror followed by giggles of
joy, relief
Zany hijinks full of excitement and awe, make
this my time of year!

Time to be You

You can be anything you want to be
It is really that easy, believe me!
Your place to shine in all your glory
The moment is now, time is ticking
Move that butt, get it in gear
Focusing clearly on the legitimacy
For the most vital part of this odyssey
Is sweet wonderful you...yes you!
It is you in charge of life's journey
Stop looking around, seeking others validity
Please try to understand this life is yours
It is fantastic, magical, beautiful you
Who has all the power within your anatomy
To create exactly what you want and need
Just give it a go, please give it a try
I will be here cheering by your side!

Phoenix Raising

Doing what you asked for
Leaves you simply infuriated
Threats and intimidation with swagger
Does not leave you gratified
Satisfaction you want or need
Power and control over me
You simply can no longer receive
So full of hate, fire, and aggression
How do you see the glorious forest?
While beating your head against that tree
Lies, empty threats, trying more manipulation
Only shines a spotlight on your own projections
Spiraling rapidly out of control
Shows your strengths and determination
I only hoped you would use them to grow
I will nurture, love, and thrive abundantly
Boldly with grace, truth, and pride
You cannot rewrite history, as hard as you try
I will continue to put in the work on this journey
Creating the life you never wanted to share with
me

Lil Big Miss

An old soul full of empathy and intuition
Always the artist creating with bursts of
pigmentation
Exquisite watercolors magnificent drips and
granulation
Brave, wicked smart, full of drive and ambition
Thrives hiking in the forest, dancing to her own
beat
Music in her ears, can't help but move her feet
Quiet and contemplating, the fresh air revives
her soul
Cracking jokes, hilarious, her laugh steals the
show
Aesthetic of dark academia, grunge, and
Victorian
She fills my heart with pride, love, respect, and
glory in
Loves horror and anime, full of unique style that
just flows
Always thoughtful, kind, and looking for life's
rainbows
So very blessed you chose me for your journey
I've loved you far longer than you were known
to me

Lil Lil Miss

Jumping, splashing in muddy puddles brings her
pure joy
Full of life, bubbly, unstoppable, ever ready to
deploy
Giggling, dancing, laughing, forever playing and
chatting
Curious, energetic, mischievous…little feet
always pit-a-patting
Princesses and superheroes are the options she
wants to be
Peppa Pig, Anna, Elsa, Mr. Beast and Spy
Ninjas her cup of tea
Tea parties and dress up, bouncing at the
Trampoline Park
Swimming, finishing puzzles, chasing rainbows,
playing till dark
Loves to hang-out, eating ice cream, pizza and
French fries
Mommy backpack time is so cozy with my
beloved pint-size
Big imagination, so very clever, vibrant,
fearless, and kind
You fill my soul with love, pride, laughs, and
magnificent sunshine
So very blessed you chose me for your journey

I've loved you far longer than you were known
to me

Ego vs Soul

Ego protects self from pain
Self-reflection causes shame
Seeking fame, constant validation
Interrupting every conversation
Only to enhance self-image
Disagree, boy you're in for a scrimmage
Can never obtain what the soul owns
This causes plenty of thrown stones
External validations, greed, superficial
Viewing people as objects, sacrificial
Ego cannot recognize wrong-doing

Soul vs Ego

Soul serves others in world viewing
People pleasing, stocked with ambition
Empath, looks inward, full of intuition
Altruism, full of compassion, humble
Self-acceptance even after a few stumbles
Has gratitude, love, working on healing
Evolving, creating, becoming whole very
appealing
Soul delicious prey for ego, easy mark
Soul pure reflection of spirit, even in the dark
Soul lives in love, ego lives in fear and control
Enlightenment, peace, authentic being soul goals

Self-Care

Mornings for running hot baths
Forging new neural paths
Salt, joy, and bubbles
Letting go of past troubles
Early mornings up to write
No longer diminishing my light
Forgiveness for yours truly
Freedom from who treated me cruelly
Respecting my weather pattern with grace
Proper rest, fresh eating becoming commonplace
Honoring my true self with each meeting
Curiosity and exploration my greeting
Purging negativity, creating my safe place
Mindfulness, creating a new knowledge base
Unapologetically evolving and growing
Nature, forest hikes, treehouses, oceangoing
Extinct living in freeze, fight, flight, or fawn
Wise mind, being present, focusing on a new
dawn

Little Things

It only took one iota
A piece of art hung ineptly
Astonished my logic and reason
To realize it's the little things
That have the ability and force
To soften, soothe my soul, bring joy
That first cup of tea or coffee
Toasting the sun as it peeks up
Over the rugged desert mountains
Emphasizing it's a glorious fresh start
Smoke rising from snug fireplaces
Mingling with crisp fall breezes
Vibrant leaves drifting into piles
Remind me it's unavoidable to let go
Good morning wake up snuggles
Groans, giggles, content sighs
Head burrowing into my arm and side
Remind me just how fast life speeds by
My wall is full now, no room to spare
Bursting with magic, kindness, peace of mind
Little things evolve, grow, and expand
Into the big things that help me understand

Time at the Shop

Searching to add to the collection
Their faces light up with affection
Ashtrays, dragons, and decanters
Saturday mornings old souls banter
Haegar, California pottery, art glass
Mid Century Modern looking to add high-class
Pyrex, cast iron, and Barbie dolls
Can you help me find pixie elves to deck my
halls?
Such joy and nostalgia the moment they find
Items from long ago, that brings grandma to
mind
Stained glass, skeleton keys, walls full of art
Who knew inanimate objects could fill your
heart?
Creepy dolls, apothecary spoons, and crystals
Figurines, antique books, black powder pistols
Let me show you something over here...
Keys please! Yes, bring it up to the cashier
Joy and jubilation early mornings at the shop

Dear Miss Me

I am so fucking proud of you
Overcoming each hand, with versions that grew
Strong will, persistence, and determination
Self-love, compassion, growth all new
foundation
Understanding that the constant people pleasing
While brief joy grew, at a great price, our soul
was seizing
Shrinking, stagnant, becoming so very small
Allowing the dark triad to make us their rag doll
Depression and self reflections in the bottom of
that hole
Brought forth pure will, strength, understanding
of my soul
I am the only one in control of my journey up
this cliff
Remembering to stop, rest, glance behind only
if...
I need to see how far I've come along
I am fucking glorious, magical, wonderfully
strong
Badass, always evolving and enough
Full of love, empathy, and creating from raw
stuff
Keep pushing, be you always and forever
It is really better late than never

Looking Back Now that I'm Here

What a journey this has been
Through abuse, pain, and sorrow...can't help but grin
Realizing the love, isn't true love when
Gaslighting, intimidation, harsh words spin
My head right around in confusion and distraction
Trying to make me small, when you were blinded by the chain reaction
Like a phoenix rising from the ashes
I have the power, control...your manipulation crashes
I decide, have my fate in my hands
No longer willing to fold under your commands
I am worthy of so much more then you believed
New ever evolving version of me conceived
Rawr…I will take up all the space I need
My soul unchained, rested, now freed